# Tropes: A Quick Reference Guide

## First Edition

Nancy C. Walker

# Table of Contents

# Disclaimers:

I have included all the tropes that my research has found at the time of writing this edition. I am not making a judgment about the moral, legal, or political issues involved with each trope.

I have attempted to make this book as accessible as possible to anyone using it. However, some tropes may be uncomfortable to read about. Be thoughtful when choosing tropes for your work.

Some tropes are specific to a certain race, sexual orientation, or gender. In those cases, the listing uses the commonly accepted terminology for the trope. Please remember that as an author, you have the power to subvert the trope to fit your story.

New tropes are constantly being created. I welcome anyone who has a suggestion for a trope to contact me via my website, NancyCWalker.com, and I will consider it for the next edition of the book.

To everyone who ever struggled with knowing
what to write. You are my people.

# What is a Trope?

Tropes are common themes, plots, and characters that we all recognize in a story. They establish our expectations for how the story will flow or how the characters will behave. While this can provide a sense of familiarity with the story, it can also become cliché if it is blatantly obvious. To avoid this, authors will subvert tropes by changing a well-established element, which creates tension and surprise.

Many people link tropes to specific genres. I present tropes on their own to force the author to see the trope as an element of story, not of genre. We can adapt tropes and subvert them to fit our stories. Ultimately, the best way to use tropes is to experiment and find what works best for you and your story.

# How to use this book

This book is an alphabetical listing of tropes with a simple description to help writers who need inspiration or want a quick reference. I listed the tropes alphabetically to make them easier to find if you already know the trope you are looking for.

If you are looking for inspiration, then browsing through the pages may spark an idea or provide a story prompt. String a few tropes together to have the start of an outline or a story prompt.

# A

**AI (Artificial Intelligence)** - Plots and themes involve the use of AI. This is a generalized trope with several sub-tropes.

**AI Helper (Assistant)** - A chatbot or program that helps the user.

**AI is Sentient** - Artificial Intelligence develops its own emotions and autonomy as a species.

**AI Villain** - Artificial intelligence that becomes the villain of the story.

**Abandoned location** - A location that is remote and neglected.

**Abduction as Seduction** - A character kidnaps another to seduce them.

**Above the Law** - A character does not receive consequences for their actions, because the law does not apply to them.

**Absence Makes the Heart Grow Fonder** - The act of separation makes two people want each other more.

**Absence of Evidence is Evidence** - The lack of evidence becomes evidence.

**Absent Murderer** - The murderer is not present at the time the victim is murdered.

**Absent Parents** - The parents of a minor are alive, but rarely if ever are mentioned in the story.

**Abuse** - This trope covers all aspects of abuse and recovery. There are several sub-tropes involving specific aspects of abuse.

**Abuse Mistake** - A character sees something between the protagonist and love interest and mistakenly thinks its abuse.

**Action Politician** - A politician who does his own "dirty work".

**Age Differences** - A significant age difference between main characters who are not in a romantic relationship.

**Age Gap** - When two romantically involved characters have an age difference of 10 or more years.

**Age Regression** - An adult becomes a child mentally because of an injury or severe trauma. An adult becomes a physical child.

**Alcoholic** - A person who is reliant on alcohol to function.

**Alien** - A creature is from a planet other than earth.

**Aliens Make Them Have Sex** - Aliens force humans to have sex with each other or with the aliens.

**All Talk, No Action** - The author tells the reader what qualities the character has, but the character never shows those qualities.

**Alone in the Building** - A character is alone in a building which implies they are about to be a victim.

**Alone with the Victim** - A character is alone with the victim, implying to the other characters that they may be the killer.

**Alpha Bitch** - A popular female character who is mean, manipulative, and entitled.

**Alpha Male** - A male character who is sexy, possessive, and dominant, but also a gentleman with ethics or a moral code.

**Alphahole** - A male character who pushes the traits of an Alpha Male to a place of violence and negativity.

**Am-badass-ador** - A diplomat who will resort to violence if needed.

**Amazons** - A race of women who are physically strong.

**Ambassador** - A diplomat who represents a country in negotiations with other countries.

**Amnesia** - Memory loss often caused by an accident or severe trauma.

**Ancient Magical Artifact** - An item from long

ago has magical powers.

**Ancient Secrets** - An ancient society has secrets which apply to the plot.

**"And Another Thing"** - When a character turns to leave, but then turns back to make a statement or ask a question.

**Angels** - Heavenly beings often associated with religion or God.

**Angry Bitch** - An angry woman who is mean, manipulative, and entitled.

**Animals as People/ Anthropomorphism** - Animals are given human traits and emotions.

**Annoying Reporter** - A newsperson who insists on antagonizing the protagonist.

**Antagonist Lust for the Heroine** - The antagonist is sexually or romantically attracted to the heroine.

**Antagonist Turned Ally** - The antagonist becomes an ally to the protagonist.

**Anti-Hero** - A character who does the wrong thing for the right reasons.

**Anti-Villain** - A character who does the right thing for the wrong reasons.

**Arranged Marriage** - When two people are set up to marry by a third party, often family or someone with control over them.

**Ass in Ambassador** - An ambassador who is unethical or rude.

**Asshole Victim** - The victim behaves in such a way that they are not liked.

**Ass Kicking Leads to Leadership** - A theme where the act of physical violence leads to a character becoming a leader.

**Astral Plane** - A state of consciousness accessed through meditation or dreams.

**Asylum** - A place where the mentally ill are sent for treatment that is often considered haunted or associated with abuse.

**At War with Aliens** - Humans are fighting beings from a place other than Earth.

**At War with Another Country** - Plots and themes involve two countries fighting with each other.

**Athlete** - A character who participates in sports.

**Auction** - An event where people bid on something that is for sale.

# B

**Bad Boyfriend** - The protagonist's boyfriend is self-fish, rude, or obviously disinterested in the relationship.

**Bad Weather** - A severe weather event that impacts the plot.

**Badass Bureaucrat** - A politician who will resort to violence if needed.

**Bait and Switch** - When one item is offered and then switched with another at the time of sale.

**Bars** - A modern setting where characters meet to be social or get information about the plot.

**Beast** - A character who is animalistic because of a medical experiment or magic spell.

**Beauty and the Beast** - The themes and plot of the story are similar to the classic fairytale.

**Bed and Breakfast** - A place that offers a place to sleep and have breakfast, often a converted home.

**Beneath Suspicion** - A character that presents as someone who would not be suspected of committing the crime in question.

**Best Friend** - The best friend of the protagonist.

**Best Friend's Ex** - The protagonist has a

romantic relationship with their best friend's ex-boyfriend or ex-husband.

**Best Friend's Sibling** - The protagonist has a romantic relationship with their best friend's sibling.

**Bet** - A character places a wager on the outcome of an event or challenge.

**Beta Bitch** - A character who is the best friend of, and often submissive to, the Alpha Bitch

**Betrayal** - A character is disloyal to another character.

**Big City Girl in a Small Town** - A woman who has always lived in the city moves to a small town and has trouble adjusting to small town life.

**Big Friendly Guy** - A male character who is physically intimidating because of his size but friendly.

**Big Guy** - Part of the five-man band, the big guy is physically strong but often not smart.

**Biker** - A character who is a part of a motorcycle club.

**Billionaire** - A character with a lot of money.

**Bisexual** - A character who is sexually attracted to more than one gender.

**Bitchy Rich Woman** - A wealthy woman who is mean, manipulative, and entitled.

**Black and White Morality** - Things in the story are good or evil.

**Black Best Friend** - A character whose identity is limited to being the protagonist's best friend and being a token minority.

**Blackmail** - When a character threatens to expose a secret if they are not given what they want.

**Blind Date** - Two characters go on a date that is organized by a third party.

**Bluffing the Kidnapper** - The protagonist deceives the kidnapper by telling them they can or will do something.

**Bluffing the Murderer** - The protagonist deceives the murderer by telling them they can or will do something.

**Body Count Competition** - Two characters compete to see who can kill the most.

**Body Horror** - Showcasing grotesque or psychologically disturbing violations to the human body.

**Bodyguard** - A person who physically protects other characters.

**Boho Chick (Hippie)** - A female character known for her quirky fashion sense, free spirit, positive perspective, deeply held beliefs, and a strong sense of self.

**Bondage is Bad** - A theme where only villains or evil characters enjoy bondage.

**Book Burning** - The literal burning of books to promote censorship or societal control.

**Boss/ Employee Relationship** - A romantic or sexual relationship between an employee and their supervisor or boss.

**Bound and Gagged** - A person is tied up and gagged to prevent them from escaping.

**Boy Next Door** - A male character who is friendly but has no distinct qualities.

**Brains and Bondage** - A theme where smart people prefer bondage or kink.

**Break the Fourth Wall** - When the protagonist speaks directly to the audience.

**Bully** - A person who is mean and/or abusive to another person.

**Bury Your Gays** - The gay character needlessly dies. This is a subtle implication that the death of gays is irrelevant.

**But It Was Poisoned** - A character is confused after another character ingests a poisoned item but does not die.

**Byronic Hero** - A character is confused after another character ingests a poisoned item but does not die.

# C

**Cabin** - A wooden structure in the woods.

**Caligula** - A psychopathic man-child.

**Camp** - A wooded location with tents or cabins.

**Camping** - Staying in the woods by choice for recreation.

**Campy (Camp)** - A style of writing that exaggerates themes and stereotypes.

**Can't Communicate** - When a character constantly misunderstands or thinks something else is being said.

**Cannibal** - A person who eats people.

**Carnival** - A temporary event with rides and food.

**Castle** - Often the home of royalty, a castle is a large structure popular in medieval Europe.

**Censorship** - Characters within the story discover they are being censored.

**Chain of Command** - The hierarchy of military leaders.

**Character Description in a Mirror** - The reader learns about a character's appearance because the character is looking in a mirror.

**Character Eating Alone** - A character eats alone to imply the character does not have friends.

**Character From a Different Time Uses Language from Modern Times** - A character modern language, when the story is set in a different time.

**Character With Vital Info Dies** - A character with important information dies before sharing the information.

**Charming/ Charismatic Villain** - The villain is charismatic.

**Cheating** - When a married character is disloyal to their partner by having sex with another person.

**Chessmaster** - A character who is the mastermind of the events in a story.

**Chief Executive Officer (CEO)** - The person who is the highest authority in the company.

**Chosen One** - A character who is chosen by fate or destiny to be the hero.

**Christian** - The story focuses on Christian themes.

**Christmas Miracle** – A major element of the plot, regardless of how improbable, happens in time for Christmas Day.

**Church** - A place for religious worship.

**Cinnamon Roll** - A male character who is sweet,

supportive, and gentle, occasionally to the point of being unrealistic.

**Circus** - A temporary event known for acrobats, animals, and shows.

**City** - A location with a lot of people and buildings.

**City Life** - Themes in the story involve things that are unique to living in a city.

**Cliffhanger** - When end of a story leaves some plot threads unfinished.

**Closed Room Mystery** - Characters are in a closed room when something happens, making them all the only suspects.

**Clown** - A person often associated with the circus who wears bright colors and makeup.

**Colonial America** - A time period in American History when the US was a group of 13 colonies.

**Comatose (Coma)** - A character is unconscious. Often, the character has vital information.

**Comic Relief Character** - A character who is humorous or silly and lightens the mood of a story.

**Coming of Age** - The story explores themes related to transitioning to an adult.

**Coming Out** - The protagonist discovers they are part of the LGBTQ+ community.

**Communication Does Not Work** - Something keeps the characters from communicating

**Communication Technology Fails** - Items used for communication fail, often because they are broken.

**Confession to Protect the Culprit** - An innocent character confesses to a crime to protect the person who they think is guilty.

**Congress** - The group of people who make laws in the US.

**Conspiracy Theorist** - A person who believes conspiracy theories.

**Conspiracy Theory** - The belief that a secret group is manipulating major events.

**Convicted by Public Opinion** - When a person is found guilty by society, even if the law finds them innocent.

**Cornering the Hero** - The villain shows his power by trapping the hero in a no-win situation.

**Corrupt Politician** - An unethical politician.

**Corrupt President** - An unethical president.

**Corsets are Sexy** - Characters wear corsets as a show of sex appeal.

**Cosmic Horror** - When a character knows something forbidden, and the information makes them insane.

**Costume Porn** - Extensive descriptions of clothing.

**Country Folk** - Characters who are in or from the country.

**Country Life** - Themes of the story involve things that are unique to living in a country.

**Cowboy** - A male character whose job is herding cattle.

**Cowgirl** - A female character who dresses in western wear and can usually shoot well.

**Crappy Carnival** - A carnival with boring rides and bad food.

**Creepy Kid** - A child or pre-teen who is creepy.

**Criminal Consultant** - A criminal who is now a consultant helping catch criminals.

**Critical Parents** - The protagonist's parents are overly critical of the protagonist or their love interest.

**Cult** - A small group of people who follow a charismatic leader and convince members to believe anything the leader says.

**Cultists** - Members of a cult.

**Cultural Conflict** - The story focuses on the clash between modern society and the protagonist's culture.

**Cultural Traditions and Customs** - An exploration of a group's culture, traditions, or customs.

**Culture-Based Hero** - The hero's identity is tied to his ethnicity or religion.

**Cursed Item** - An item is cursed and the protagonist is affected by the curse.

**Cursed Person** - A character is cursed and must break it.

**Cursed Place** - A location with a curse.

**Cut Himself Shaving** - A character with a suspicious wound provides a plausible, if unbelievable, excuse.

**Cyborg** - The story focuses on characters who are half man - half machine.

# D

**DL Jock** - A male character who presents as overtly masculine, but is secretly gay.

**Daddy Dom** - A dominant character who takes on a parental role for their submissive.

**Damage Tolerance** - A character has an unrealistically high tolerance for taking damage.

**Dame with a Case** - A woman walks in with a case that needs to be solved.

**Damsel** - A young woman with typically feminine traits.

**Damsel in Distress** - A woman is in danger and needs the help of a male character.

**Dare** - A character challenges another character.

**Dark Lord** - A character who is evil because they enjoy being evil.

**Dark Misunderstood Guy** - A male character who is presumed to be a villain because of his dark traits.

**Dating Apps** - Characters use dating apps.

**Death to Sinners** - All the characters who commit sins die.

**Decadent Emperor** - An emperor who is more interested in his wealth than ruling.

**Demons** - A creature commonly stated to be from Hell and working as a servant of the devil.

**Demons Have Feelings** - Demons are characters with feelings and human qualities.

**Detective** - A character who solves mysteries.

**Detective Denouement** - When all the clues are stated by the detective at the end of a story.

**Detective Drama** - While solving the mystery, the detective learns the mystery involves him.

**Detective with Substance Abuse Issue** - The detective is addicted to alcohol or drugs.

**Deus ex Machina** - When an unsolvable problem is suddenly solved because of a sudden or unexpected help.

**Doctor** - A character who is a doctor.

**Dominant (Dom)** - A male character who is in control during a BDSM relationship.

**Dominatrix** - A female character who is in control during a BDSM scene.

**Domme** - A female character who is in control during a BDSM relationship.

**"Don't Die on Me"** - A character who is dying miraculously lives after being told not to die.

**Doppelgänger** - An unrelated person who looks extremely similar to another person.

**Double Cross** - When a person betrays someone who they were supposedly working with.

**Dressed In Latex** - A person wears latex to show they are part of the BDSM community.

**Dressed Like a Dominatrix** - A person dressed to look like a dominatrix.

**Drifter Cowboy** - A cowboy who moves from ranch to ranch to find work.

**Driving Question** - The main question the hero is trying to answer.

**Dubious Consent (Dub-con)** - When a character coerces an unwilling character to do something.

**Dude Ranch** - A ranch where tourists can dress up and pretend to be cowboys.

**Dude Ranch Cowboy** - A cowboy who runs a dude ranch.

**Dumb Blonde** - Blonde characters, often females, are portrayed as lacking intelligence.

**Dumb Jock** - An athlete who is great at sports but lacks basic intelligence.

**Duo Relationship** - The focus of the story is on two people and their non-romantic relationship to each other.

**Dystopian** - A near future world in which the ruling class are tyrants and society accepts unjust ideals.

# E

**Early Suspect** - The character suspected of the crime early on. Often, they are a red herring.

**Emperor with an Agenda** - An emperor who has an obsessive goal.

**Employee** - A person who works for a company.

**Empty Shell** - A character whose soul is gone but their lifeless body continues to function.

**Enemies Forced to Work Together** - People who don't like each other are required to work together to complete a task.

**Enemies to Lovers** - Two people who dislike each other fall in love.

**Ethnic Hero/ Heroine** - One or more protagonists' ethnicity or cultural traditions are a plot point of the story.

**Eureka Moment** - The protagonist has an idea that is crucial to the plot.

**Everybody Did It** - All the suspects committed the crime together.

**Everyone Is a Suspect** - All the characters are considered suspects in the story.

**Evidence Scavenger Hunt** - The characters look for clues to a mystery or crime.

**Evil Alien Race** - A specific race of aliens whose purpose in the story is to be a blank, evil force.

**Evil Boss** - An employer who is mean-spirited and cruel.

**Evil Boyfriend** - A boyfriend who is mean-spirited and cruel.

**Evil Empire** - An empire that embodies everything the hero is not.

**Evil Mentor** - A mentor who is mean-spirited and cruel.

**Evil Overlord** - An overlord who is mean-spirited and cruel.

**Evil Plan** - A plan that is devious or has the intent to be malicious.

**Evil Prince** - A prince who is mean-spirited and cruel.

**Evil Returns** - Something bad that everyone thought was over comes back.

# F

**Fairy** - Creatures known for having wings and magical powers.

**Fake Alibis Discovered** - The protagonist learns an alibi is fake.

**Fake Death** - Someone pretends they are dead.

**Fake Engagement** - Two people pretend to be engaged.

**Fake Spouse** - Two people pretend they are married to each other.

**Fallen Bitch** - A mean woman who has fallen out with the rest of her friends.

**Fallen Empire** - The ruling, often evil, empire is destroyed.

**Fallen Hero** - When the hero becomes the villain.

**Family** - A group of people who are related by DNA.

**Family Drama** - Plots and themes focus on the relationships between family members.

**Farm** - A place with animals and crops.

**Farmboy** - A young man becomes the hero of the story, even though he has lived his whole life sheltered on a farm.

**Feeling of Being Watched** - The protagonist gets the feeling someone is watching them.

**Femme Fatale** - A female who uses her charm and intelligence to manipulate the male protagonist.

**Fetishes are Weird** - The implication that people who have fetishes are not normal.

**Fight for the Throne** - The protagonist and their siblings fight to see who will take the throne after their ruling parent dies or goes missing.

**Fighter Pushed Too Far** - A character who is pushed beyond their physical limits and it shows.

**Fighting for Love** - The protagonist's motivation for fighting is because they are in love.

**Final Girl** - The last girl alive at the end of a story or battle. Often, she is also the least likely to be alive.

**Finding Old Footage/ Photographs** - A clue to a mystery is in an old video or photo.

**First Love** - The protagonist has their first love, or is hung up on their first love, making them incapable of moving on.

**Fish Out of Water** - The protagonist is awkward in a new setting.

**Five Man Band** - A common character trope of

five people. Hero, Lancer, Smart Guy, Big Guy, Heart (Chick).

**Flying Cities** - Cities that are floating above the planet.

**Force of Nature** - A character who will stop at nothing to achieve their goals, often leaving chaos in their wake like a major storm.

**Forced Proximity** - Two characters are stuck together because of an outside force.

**Forest** - A place with a lot of trees.

**Forgotten Children** - When the story is about a single parent, but the children are rarely mentioned and never seen.

**Found Family** - A group that comes together and is supportive of each other in the way a family should be. Often, they have a shared culture or tradition that ties them together.

**Frenemies** - Two people who pretend to be enemies in public but friends in private.

**Friends as Parents** - When a parent acts more like a friend than a parent.

**Friends to Lovers** - Two characters who are friends become lovers.

**Funny Fat Girl** - An overweight female character is presented as the funny character that other often make fun of.

# G

**Gay Best Friend** - A character whose identity is limited to being the protagonist's best friend and stereotypically gay.

**Gay Conservative** - A gay person with traditionally conservative values.

**Gay for You** - A heterosexual person who declares they would become gay for a specific person.

**Gendered Name is Gender Neutral** – The protagonist assumes a character is a specific gender based on their name, only to discover the name is gender neutral and their presumption is wrong.

**Ghost** - The spirit of a dead person.

**Ghost in the Mirror** - A ghost is trapped in a mirror.

**Ghost Town** - An abandoned town, often it is haunted.

**Girl Next Door** - A female character who is friendly but has no distinct qualities.

**Glasses are Ugly** - A female character gets contact lenses to show that she is now beautiful.

**Godlike Aliens** - Aliens are worshiped as if they were gods.

**Gods** - Heavenly beings with a lot of power.

**Good Girl Gone Bad** - A female character who is usually well behaved and "good" changes into a poorly behaved "bad" character.

**Good Girl/ Bad Boy** - A strait-laced female and law-breaking male fall in love.

**Good Guys are Invincible** - The main characters fight a major battle but suffer no trauma, injuries, or deaths.

**Good v. Evil** - A common trope where good and evil fight.

**Governmental Procedure** - The process by which the government works.

**Graveyard** - A place where the dead are buried.

**Gray Morality** - Bad things happen for good reasons.

**Grieving Lover** - The protagonist is grieving the death of their lover and is unable to move on to new relationships.

**Grieving Person** - The protagonist is grieving the death of a person and is unable to move on to new relationships.

**Grimdark** - A tone or style that is dark, violent, serious.

**Grizzled Older Character** - A serious older character who has had hard life experiences.

Often a veteran of war.

**Grocery Store** - A place to purchase groceries or stock up.

**Group of Friends** - The story has multiple protagonists who are all moving through their own love story within the same book or series.

**Grumpy Sunshine** - A grumpy character and a happy character have a romantic relationship.

**Grumpy Usurper** - A ruler who killed all the other heirs or who had them exiled in order to take over the empire/ company.

**Guardian** - A person responsible for the physical protection of another.

# H

**Hardened Badass** - A female character who is tough, uncompromising, and who adopts traditionally male traits. This trope is a more intense version of the Tomboy.

**Harem** - A group of women who all have the same male lover/ spouse. The female characters are not romantically involved with each other.

**Haunted House** - A house with ghosts.

**Hear no Evil** - The monster controls others through sound.

**Heart (Chick)** - Part of the five-man band trope, the heart is the emotional peacekeeper of the group. This role is often played by a female and sometimes referred to as "the chick".

**Heartless** - A character who is mean and malevolent because of experiences or because their soul has been removed.

**Heir** - The protagonist is going to inherit money, possessions, or power from a relative when they die.

**Hell** - The place where bad people go after they are dead, typically where Satan rules.

**"Here Comes the Cavalry "** - A character states this to show that others are coming to help the protagonist.

**Hero** - A character who does the right thing for the right reason.

**Hero (Five Man Band)** - The hero is the leader of the five-man band trope.

**Hero Dies** - The hero of the story dies.

**Hero Survives** - The hero survives an event that should have killed them.

**Hero Thinks They Won, But Did Not** - The hero believes they won a fight only to discover that they lost in another way.

**Hero's Journey (Monomyth)** - A structural trope created by Joseph Campbell. The hero goes on an adventure and learns a moral lesson before returning home.

**Heroic Sacrifice** - When the hero sacrifices themselves in order to win a battle or conflict.

**Hidden Identity** - The protagonist hides their real identity from someone else.

**Hidden in Plain Sight** - An item that the protagonist is looking for ends up being plainly visible the whole time.

**Hidden Power** - The protagonist hides their magical or super powers.

**Hidden Treasure** - A treasure is hidden somewhere and the protagonist has to find it.

**Hidden Villain** - The identity of the villain is revealed later in the story.

**High Fantasy** - A fantasy story where the world does not resemble real life.

**High School** - A place where teens are educated.

**Hired Muscle** - Strong men hired by the antagonist to attack the protagonist.

**Historical** - A story that focuses on themes and situations from the past.

**History Repeats** - A theme from the past is repeated

**Holiday** - A story that focuses on a particular holiday, most often Christmas.

**Homogeneous Species** - A group that has indistinguishable features between the individual creatures.

**Honor Marriage** - Two characters marry to protect one or both of their reputations.

**Horror** - Plots and themes are intended to scare or disturb the reader.

**Hospital** - A place where people get medical care.

**Hot But Doesn't Know It** - The heroine is conventionally beautiful but isn't aware of their beauty.

**Hotel** - A large building with several rooms

where people stay temporarily. Note: Individual rooms are accessed from the interior of the main building.

**Hyper Focused Character** - A character who has a single focus that drives their development through the story.

# I

**I Can't Kill A Bad Guy** - The hero makes the moral decision to not kill someone who deserves it.

**"I Never Said…"** (Spoken by the protagonist) - A character claims the protagonist told them something when they didn't. Often this is used as evidence of the character's guilt.

**"I Never Said …"** (Spoken by the suspect) - When a character reveals that they know something they shouldn't.

**"I'll Be Right Back"** - A character says they are going to return, but never does.

**Ice Queen** - A female ruler known for being ruthless and heartless.

**Identical Twins** - Two people who look exactly alike.

**Ignore My Feelings** - A character ignores their feelings for another person or has their feelings ignored by someone they like romantically.

**iMother** - A feminine chatbot or program characterized by their lack of sexualization. It is the opposite of a Smart Sex Object.

**In Medias Res** - When the story starts in the middle of an action sequence.

**In Plain Sight** - A clue is easily spotted because it's in the open.

**Incest** - When two characters who are directly related have sex.

**Incompetent Police Officer** - A cop who can't do their job.

**Infection** - A concoction often used to make people sick or turn them into zombies.

**Injured Animal** - The protagonist cares for a permanently injured animal as an allegory for caring for humans with physical or mental challenges.

**Inn** - A place that offers a place to sleep. Considered cozier than a hotel.

**Insta-Love** - When two characters fall in love instantly.

**Instructor/ Student Relationship** - An instructor and student have a romantic or sexual relationship.

**Intelligent Villain** - A villain who is intelligent.

**Interrupted Confession/ Announcement** - A character is interrupted when they are confessing or making an important announcement

**Invincibility** - The protagonist cannot be hurt.

**Invisible President** - The president of a country is referenced but not seen on the page.

**Irrelevant Love Interest** - The love interest is only there so the story can have a love interest. They are not relevant to character development or the plot.

**Isolated Location** - A place with no people or traffic.

**Issue Drift** - When the story gets away from the main topic.

**It Was All A Dream** - At the end of the story, it is revealed that the whole thing was a dream.

# J

**Jock** - An athlete who is particularly good at sports.

**Join Me** - The villain suggests that the hero join him and give up being good.

**Just One Bed** - Two characters need a place to sleep but the hotel only has one bed left.

# K

**Kawaii Characters** - Sexually mature female characters with high-pitched voices and childlike personalities.

**Kidnapped** - The protagonist is taken against their will by others.

**Kids Playing Matchmaker** - A single parent's children set them up to date a person the children like.

**Kiju** - The monsters are the size of skyscrapers.

**Killer is the Detective** - The person investigating the crime turns out to be the killer.

**King** - The male ruler of a country.

# L

**LGBTQ+** - Plots and themes relevant to the LGBTQ+ community

**Labyrinth** - A maze, often built from hedges, that the protagonist must find their way through.

**Lancer** - Part of the five-man band trope, the lancer is the second in command and has the opposite personality of the hero.

**Larger Than Life Character** - A character who is overly dramatic and over the top.

**Larger Than Life Threat** - A threat to the protagonist that is overly dramatic and over the top.

**Laser Swords in Space** - The story occurs in space and all the swords are laser based.

**Lich** - A magical being that uses magic to defy death.

**Lies** - Significant plot points involve the characters lying to each other.

**Lightbulb Moment** - When the protagonist has an epiphany about the plot.

**Lights Off, Somebody Dies** - When the lighting goes dark, someone dies.

**Linear Plot Lines** - When the story follows

several characters who have their own plotlines. Often the

plots merge at the end.

**Locked Room Mystery** - The mystery, often a murder, happens in a room that was locked. This limits the suspects to those in the room.

**Lone Cowboy** - A cowboy who runs his ranch by himself.

**Loner** - The protagonist prefers to be alone as a symbol of being lonely.

**Loss of Innocence** - When a character who is seen as having childlike purity has something happen and they lose that status.

**Loss of Mentor** - The mentor disappears or dies, affecting the protagonist.

**Lost Evidence** - The evidence of a crime is lost by law enforcement or the detective.

**Love** - Love is a theme in the story.

**Love and Loss** - The theme of the story is that someone falls in love and then loses that love.

**Love Interest** - The person the protagonist falls in love with.

**Love Triangle** - Two characters are romantically interested in the same person.

**Low Fantasy** - A fantasy story that occurs in a

modern setting.

**Lucky Novice** - A character easily wins a game or contest despite being new to playing.

# M

**Machine Worship** - The worship of machines.

**Mad Scientist** - A scientist who is chaotic and unpredictable.

**Mafia** - Plots and themes related to organized crime.

**Magic (Supernatural)** - The protagonist has supernatural powers.

**Magical Books** - A book is a portal to another location literally or because the character dreams about it, thus experiencing it.

**Magical Loopholes** - A problem in the magical system that allows the hero to use magic in ways that is not intended by the established rules of the magical system.

**Makeover** - The protagonist changes from ugly to pretty through superficial changes

**Maniac Emperor** - A chaotic ruler who rules through fear

**Maniac Empress** - A female rule who is cruel and often tries to seduce the hero.

**Manic Pixie Dream Girl** - A female character who is beautiful, energetic to the point of hyperactive, quirky, and has a childlike enthusiasm.

**Marriage of Convenience** - Two characters marry for reasons other than love.

**Marriage Pact** - Two friends promise to marry each other if they haven't found love by a certain date or age.

**Mary Sue** - A self-insert character based on the author.

**Masked Villain** - A villain whose identity is hidden from the protagonist by a mask, makeup, or a disguise.

**Masks and Weapons** - The bad guys all have masks and weapons.

**Mastering Difficult Skills Easily** - The protagonist quickly masters skills that should take months.

**Matchmaker Falls in Love** - A matchmaker falls in love with one of her clients or a person playing matchmaker for a friend, falls in love with the friend.

**Maze** - A maze the protagonist has to find their way through.

**McGuffin** - An object in the story that is only relevant because the protagonist needs or wants it. The object itself is irrelevant and can be changed out for any other object.

**Medical** - Plots and themes involve people, places, and things related to medicine.

**Ménage à trois** - When three characters have a sexual relationship at the same time.

**Mentor** - A character who provides information and training to the hero.

**Mercy Killing** - When a terminally ill person is killed in order to preserve their dignity or stop their suffering.

**Mermaid** - A humanoid type creature that lives in the water.

**Military** - Plots and themes involve military concepts.

**Military Base** - The location where military personnel work and live

**Millennial Activist** - A character who loudly supports all causes even if they don't understand them.

**Mind Control** - A character uses a device or magic to control the thoughts of another.

**Mirrors as Doors** - A mirror works like a door into another world.

**Mischief for Punishment** - A character acts badly because they want to be punished.

**Misdiagnosed Cause of Death** - The cause of death is wrong, sending investigators in the wrong direction.

**Missing Parent Reunion** - An estranged parent

or relative returns and wants a relationship.

**Mistaken for Evidence** - A mundane item is thought to be evidence.

**Mistaken Identity** - One character is believed to be someone else.

**Mistaken Identity Because of a Mask** - A character is thought to be someone else because they are wearing a mask.

**Mistress** - The woman a married man has a sexual relationship with that isn't his wife. Also, the title for a Domme.

**Misuse of Alien or Future Tech** - The story spends time to intricately explain a piece of tech, but then never brings it up again or it has no relevance to the story.

**Mom** - A female character who projects the typical traits of being a mother.

**Monster** - A creature known for being ugly, scary, or malevolent.

**Motel** - A large building with several rooms or A main building for checking into individual cabins where people stay temporarily. Note: Individual rooms are accessed from the exterior of the main building.

**Motorcycle Club (MC)** - A place where bikers socialize.

**Multiple Murders** - Several people are killed so the murderer can hide their intended target.

**Multiple Points of View that Come Together** - The story follows several characters who are having separate adventures then meet to have a combined adventure.

**Murder Mimics a Movie/ TV Show** - A murder follows the plot of an in-story movie or TV show.

**Murder Mimics a Video Game** - A murder follows the plot line of an in-story video game.

**Murder Mystery** - The plot of the story focuses on solving a murder by collecting clues.

**Mutant** - A human character who has been changed to give them superpowers or magical abilities. Often the tradeoff is a significant change to their physical appearance.

**Mysterious Neighbor** - A character who keeps secrets or acts strangely and lives near the protagonist.

**Mythology** - A belief system that is the underlying theme of the story.

# N

**Nanny** - A person who is hired to care for young children.

**Nerd** - A character whose traits include being academically smart, lacking social skills, and being unpopular.

**New Baby** - Plots and themes focus on having a new baby in the family.

**New Bitch** - A female character, who is new to the setting, who is mean, manipulative, and entitled.

**New Parent** - Plots and themes focus on being a new parent.

**New Person** - A new person arrives to the setting, often signaling the start of an adventure.

**New Sibling** - The protagonist discovers they have a new sibling.

**New World** - The protagonist finds a literal new world and spends time exploring it.

**Nice Guy** - A male character who is supportive of the female protagonist, but she doesn't see him as a love interest. When he isn't chosen, he becomes jealous and may turn into an antagonist.

**Nightmare** - The protagonist has a nightmare that reflects their inner turmoil.

**"No Time to Explain"** - When a character needs something to happen quickly or doesn't want to explain their reasoning.

**No Trespassing** - Characters are told not to go to a specific location, but they do it anyway, often setting off something malevolent or dangerous.

**Noble Bastard** - The illegitimate child of royalty, making them ineligible to inherit the kingdom.

**Non-Believer** - When a character tries to warn others of disaster or problems but no one believes them.

**Non-Consensual (non-con)** - When a character forces an unwilling character to do something.

**Nosy Neighbor** - A neighbor constantly tries to find out what the protagonist is doing.

**Nosy Person** - A person constantly tries to find out what the protagonist is doing.

**Nosy Reporter** - A reporter constantly tries to find out what the protagonist is doing, often so they can publish the information.

**Not a Suicide** - A characters death appears to be a suicide but it is not.

**Notable Non-Sequitur** - A character has a thought or piece of dialogue that seems random but provides a clue or exposition the reader needs.

**Nurse** - A character who works with doctors,

often in a medical setting.

# O

**Obsessive Parent** - A parent who is overly involved in the child's life. Often the child is an adult but the parent still controls everything the child does.

**Office** - A setting where the hero works a white collar or "desk" job.

**Office Party** - The hero attends a party with their co-workers.

**Office Politics** - The interactions between co-workers and their superiors as they compete for promotions.

**Office Romance** - When two co-workers have a romance.

**Omniscient Genius** - A character who is portrayed as knowing everything about everything.

**One Night Only** - A male character breaks his rule to only sleep with a woman once as a sign that he is in love.

**Online Dating** - Two characters meet or date via the Internet.

**Opposite Personalities** - One character is dark and moody while the other is bubbly and happy.

**Opposites Attract** - Two characters with opposite

personalities are attracted to each other.

**Orphaned Protagonist** - An underage protagonist is an orphan in order to avoid any complications that may arise from parental supervision.

**Overly Sexualized Female Characters** - The female characters all wear skimpy outfits and have promiscuous personalities.

**Overpowered Superhero** - The hero's powers are so strong that it's unbelievable anything would hurt them.

**Overpowered Weapon** - The main weapon is so powerful that it is the answer for every problem.

**Own Voices** - The plots and themes of the story focus on social or cultural issues experienced by the author in real life.

# P

**POC to White Love Interest Pipeline** - A minority race character has several options for a love interest but chooses a white person, even when the white person does not make sense for the character or the story.

**Paragon** - A character that shows the hero how to help themselves.

**Parallel Universe** - A universe seems similar to ours, but has subtle differences.

**Parasite** - A creature that lives by draining the life force from another.

**Parasitic Person** - A character who drains others either literally or by draining their desire to live.

**Pentagon** - US Military building where major military decisions are made.

**Person With Vital Info Dies** - A character who has vital information about the plot dies before telling the main characters.

**Pet Companion** - The protagonist has a pet for a companion.

**Philosopher Cowboy** - An intelligent person who prefers to work on a ranch than in an office.

**Pick Me Boy** - A male character who is constantly seeking attention by inserting himself into conversations or being annoying.

**Place with a History** - A location where the history is relevant to the plot.

**Plot Twist** - A sudden or unexpected shift in story that forces the reader to re-evaluate their expectations of the story.

**Police Officer** - The protagonist works in law enforcement.

**Political Correctness is Evil** - The theme of the story is to show how being politically correct causes harm.

**Politician** - A person who is involved in government.

**Politics** - Plots and themes focus on how a government works.

**Polyamory** - Multiple characters have romantic relationships with each other at the same time.

**Population Control** - The government creates rules to limit the population.

**Possessed** - A ghost or spirit takes control of the hero.

**Post Traumatic Stress Disorder (PTSD)** - A mental disorder often seen as the result of trauma or violence.

**Power Dynamic** - The hierarchy of control between characters.

**Power Dynamics Kink/ Total Power Exchange (TPE)** - A type of BDSM where one character gives control of everything to another.

**Power of Friendship** - Plots and themes focus on the benefits of friendship.

**Power of Teamwork** - Plots and themes focus on the benefits of teamwork.

**Powerful Artifact** - An item from a long-ago time that contains powerful magic.

**Powerful Children** - A child can defeat an adult or supernatural being without struggling.

**Powerful People are Submissive** - People in positions of authority in daily life are submissive in the bedroom.

**Pregnancy Pact** - A group of females all promise to be pregnant together.

**Premature Suspect** - A character is suspected of a crime before all the evidence is discovered.

**President (of a Club)** - The leader of a group or club.

**President (of a Country)** - The leader of a country.

**President Superhero** - The protagonist does something heroic which results in him becoming the president.

**Pretty Girl in a Dirty World** - A female character continues to be clean and beautiful, even though her surroundings would make that impossible.

**Price of Power** - When the protagonist must pay a price for acquiring a new power or skill. The greater the power or skill, the greater the price.

**Prince** - A male heir to the throne.

**Princess** - A female heir to the throne.

**Prisoner** - A character who is incarcerated.

**Problem Teen** - A teenage character who struggles with drugs, drinking, running away, or acting out.

**Professor/ Student** - A professor and student have a romantic or sexual relationship. Use of the term Professor implies the student is college age.

**Progression of Mankind to the Next Level** - Humans evolve into another species.

**Prom Date** - The plot of the story focuses on the protagonist having a date for the prom.

**Prop Weapon is** - A weapon that is supposed to be a prop turns out to be real.

**Propaganda** - Media that has a specific political message in order to influence the population.

**Protected by Love** - Because someone loves the protagonist, they can't be hurt or killed.

**Pseudo-Europe as Medieval** - The settings of a story set in medieval times uses inspiration from various European countries in different time periods.

**Psychological Horror** - Horror specifically involving mental and emotional conditions.

**Psychological Landscape** - The character's internal fears project onto the setting. What they see/hear may not be real or a hallucination.

**Psychopath** - A character who does not feel emotions but can mimic feelings to manipulate others.

**Psychosexual Horror** - Plots and themes explore sexual development or interests using suspense, sexual tension, and a sense of danger.

**Pulling a Sherlock** - When the protagonist solves a mystery by noticing small things that are often overlooked.

# Q

**Quests** - The protagonist must go on a journey as part of the plot, or for character development.

# R

**Rags to Riches** - The protagonist starts the story poor and becomes rich by the end.

**Rape** - A character has sex with a non-consenting partner.

**Rape Revenge** - A raped character gets revenge on their rapist.

**Realism** - When the story has the impression that it is based in real life, even when some elements may be fantastical.

**Reanimated Corpse** - A dead body can move because it is being controlled by another character.

**Recovery Drama** - Plots and themes focus on the protagonist recovering from or dealing with addiction.

**Red Herring** - A false clue or misdirection in a story.

**Redeemed Hero** - A villain who becomes a hero by changing their point of view or beliefs.

**Redemption Arc** - A bad or morally gray character becomes good.

**Religious Person** - A person who is firm in their religious beliefs.

**Religious Zealot** - A religious character who is radical in their beliefs.

**Reluctant Hero** - The hero is reluctant to accept his part in the story.

**Reluctant Ruler** - A person who ends up ruling a country or running a business because they have to, not because they want to.

**Remote Research Facility** - A setting where medical or scientific research is done. Often set in a rural area.

**Rescue Romance** - The male character rescues the female character from a physically dangerous situation.

**Resurrection** - A character is killed in the story, but miraculously comes back to life.

**Return from the Dead** - A character who was presumed to be dead for years comes back alive.

**Return to Home** - A character goes back to their hometown or childhood home and discovers something about themselves.

**Revenge** - The hero seeks vengeance on those who hurt them.

**Reverse Harem** - A group of male characters all have the same female lover/ spouse. The male characters are not romantically involved with each other.

**Reverse Whodunnit** - A story structure where the reader knows who committed the crime. The focus of the story is about how to catch the criminal, not on who did it.

**Revolutionary Villain** - The protagonist is fighting tyranny but goes too far and becomes a villain.

**Revulsion** - Making readers feel disgusted by diseased blood, gore, violence, etc.

**Rich Bitch** - A rich woman who is mean, manipulative, and entitled.

**Rich Guy** - A male character with a lot of money.

**Rival** - A character who wants the same thing as the hero, creating conflict.

**Robot Uprising** - Robots rebel against their role as servants and fight to rule over humanity.

**Rock Star** - Plots and themes focus on the main characters being popular musicians or singers.

**Rodeo Rider** - A cowboy who rides bulls.

**Romance** - Plots and themes focus on two or more characters falling in love.

**Romanticized Cheating** - When a character romantically cheats on their partner but it's written as romantic.

**Royals Who Actually Do Something** - A member of royalty who actively works or fights alongside their people.

**Royalty** - A member of the ruling class in a governmental system where leaders are chosen based on their lineage.

**Ruins of a Dead Civilization** - The location where an extinct civilization used to live.

**Runaway Bride** - The bride literally runs from her wedding. Popular plots for this trope are the bride and groom getting back together, or the bride discovering her true love after leaving her wedding.

**Rural** - Plots and themes focus on being in a rural setting.

# S

**Sadist** - A person who enjoys inflicting pain.

**Safe Word Forgotten** - A character in a BDSM scene forgets their safe word which causes tension between the characters.

**Safe, Sane, and Consensual** - Plots and themes focus on how relationships, specifically kink and BDSM, should be safe and consensual.

**Save the Cat** - When the protagonist does something to make them likable to the reader. A specific writing method involving three acts and 15 plot points.

**Saying Too Much** - A character accidentally provides clues or context to the protagonist by talking too much.

**Scientist/ Researcher Relationship** - A scientist and researcher have a romantic or sexual relationship.

**Second Chance Romance** - Plots and themes focus on two characters who previously broke up getting back together.

**Second Character Dies** - A second character is killed in the story.

**Secret Baby** - A woman hides her baby's existence from the child's father.

**Secret Billionaire** - A character hides their status as a billionaire.

**Secret Heir** - A character hides their status as the heir to a big company or royal position.

**Secret Identity** - A character adopts a second identity to hide that they are a superhero or secret agent.

**Secrets** - Plots and themes involve the characters keeping secrets from each other.

**Security Company** - A company that offers personal or professional security, mercenaries, or military type rescue services.

**See Ghosts in a Mirror** - The protagonist sees a person in a mirror, but when they turn around, the ghost is gone.

**Seduced by the Monster** - A literal monster seduces the heroine.

**See No Evil** - The monster is invisible or seeing it will cause damage/death to the protagonist.

**Serial Killings to Hide the True Target** - Several people are killed to hide that the killer wanted a specific person dead.

**Sex is Evil** - Plots and themes result in bad things happening to characters who have sex or participate in sexual acts.

**Sexy One** - A female character who dresses and

behaves to show off their sexual prowess.

**She's Just Crazy** - A female character has vital information about the plot, but no one believes her because "she's crazy".

**Shell Game** - Two nearly identical items are mixed up causing the hero to have the wrong item. This can also apply to having multiple characters who look alike and the hero having to determine which one is the real person.

**Shifters** - Human characters that can change into animals.

**Shipwrecked** - Pots and themes involve the characters being stranded after their ship or plane crashes.

**Shopping Mall** - A large complex with multiple retail and food outlets.

**Shrewd Detective** - A detective character that rarely misses anything and is often a step ahead of the other characters in solving the crime or mystery.

**Side Quests** - Smaller quests that the main characters must accomplish to get items or information for the main quest.

**Sidekick** - A secondary character who helps the hero.

**Silly One** - A female character who acts silly or childish.

**Singing Cowboy** - A cowboy who sings.

**Single Parent** - A single adult raising a child.

**Skimpy/Slutty Clothing for Women** - All the female characters wear sexually revealing clothing.

**Slacker** - A lazy character.

**Slow Burn** - When two characters slowly fall in love.

**Slut** - A sexually promiscuous female character.

**Small Town** - Plots and themes involve a town with a small population.

**Small Town Boy** - A male character from a small town moves to a big city and struggles to adapt to city life.

**Smart Guy** - Part of the five-man band, the smart guy is the one who is physically weak but mentally strong.

**Smart Sex Object** - A chatbot or program designed to flirt and lure men. It is the opposite of the iMother trope.

**Smitten Teen Girl** - A teenage girl is infatuated with the hero.

**Sociopath** - A character with a lack of remorse, shallow emotions, and a disregard for laws/ rules.

**Soldier** - A member of the military.

**Solve the Problem with Science** - The protagonist solves a problem by using science while intricately explaining it.

**Soul Mate** - A character who is fated or destined to be the love interest of another character.

**Soulless** - A character that does not have a soul because the soul has been removed or because the character lacks empathy.

**Space Station** - Plots and themes focus on living or working on a space station.

**Speak No Evil** - Saying the monster's name can summon it or the monster finds its prey through sound.

**Speed Dating** - The protagonist and love interest are involved in speed dating.

**Split Up the Group** - A group of characters split up to explore an area.

**Spy Fiction** - Plots and themes focus on things related to spying or covert operations.

**Stakeout** - When a character, usually law enforcement, watches a suspected criminal covertly.

**Stalker Romance** - A female character falls in love with her stalker.

**Stalker with a Crush** - A person who is stalking someone because they want, or believe they have, a romantic relationship with the person.

**Stalker with an Obsession** - A person who is obsessed with someone for non-romantic reasons.

**Starchild** - A variation of the Chosen One, the starchild has an innate power that makes them special and the hero of the story.

**Story in a Story** - When a character in the main story tells a story to another character.

**Stately Home** - A large home with well-trimmed gardens.

**Step-Parent** - A non-related parental figure. Often married to the related parental figure.

**Step-Sibling** - A sibling through marriage, but not directly related.

**Stripper/ Prostitute turned Respectable** - When a character in the main story tells a story to another character.

**Stranded** - The protagonist is left or stuck somewhere without working transportation.

**Strawman News** - The in-story news source is biased or only reports propaganda.

**Stuck Together** - A female character who used to be a stripper, now has a respectable job or position.

**Student** - Plots and themes focus on the protagonist being a student.

**Submissive (sub)** - A person who willingly submits to a Dom or Domme.

**Sudden Power Up** - A character suddenly has a new super power in order to win a fight.

**Suddenly Stupid** - A smart character does stupid, out of character, things to further the plot.

**Summoning Evil** - The protagonist calls on a demon in order to make a deal or use the demon's power.

**Super School** – A fantasy for sci-school that is less about academic learning and more about having adventures.

**Surprise Child** - The protagonist discovers they have a child they did not know about. This usually refers to a child who is older than two.

**Surprise Pregnancy** - A character discovers they, or someone they had sex with, are unexpectedly pregnant.

**Surprise, Not Single** - The plot includes the characters planning or trying to get married, and discovering that they are not actually single.

**Surreal Horror** - The story plays on illogical and incomprehensible fears.

**Surrounded by Monsters** - The protagonist is surrounded by monsters and appears to have no hope of survival.

**Survivalist** - A character who can survive in a wilderness setting with minimal supplies.

# T

**Talking Animals** - The personification of animals by having them talk and behave as humans.

**Tattered Flag** - A ripped up flag is discovered as a sign that the country survived the war.

**Taverns** - A medieval setting where characters meet to be social or get information about the plot.

**Teacher** - A character who works in a school and teaches minors.

**Teacher/ Student Relationship** - A teacher and student have a romantic or sexual relationship. Use of the term teacher implies the student is a minor.

**Team Dad** - The character who is usually the oldest and fills a mentor role.

**Temple** - A location with magic or religious connections.

**Terminal Illness** - Plots and themes focus on the protagonist having a terminal illness.

**Terror** - The protagonist is threatened by something ambiguous.

**The Big Reveal** - The end of the story when the murderer or criminal is revealed or the mystery is solved.

**The Butler Did It** - The murderer or criminal is a person that no one suspected because they blend into the background.

**The End, or is it?** - After the resolution, there is one last hint that the story might not be over.

**The Game Never Stopped** - The characters play a game which causes something to happen. As things continue to happen, the characters realize they are still in the game.

**The Person You Least Suspect** - The guilty person is the person least suspected by the reader.

**Time Travel** - Plots and themes focus on the protagonist's ability to travel through time.

**Token Minority** - A minority character is added to a story for the sole purpose of the author being able to claim the characters are "diverse".

**Token Political Party Member** - A character who wouldn't logically be a member of a particular political party, is a member for the sole purpose of claiming diversity.

**Tomboy** - A female character, often a child, who prefers traditionally male activities but identifies as female.

**Too Dumb to Live** - A character who wouldn't logically be a member of a particular political party, is made a member for the sole purpose of claiming diversity.

**Too Kinky to Torture** - A character who can't be tortured because they like to hurt. This plays into the idea that kink equals an enjoyment of pain.

**Toxic Friend** - A friend of the protagonist who doesn't really care about them.

**Train** - A character who can't be tortured because they like to hurt. This plays into the idea that kink equals an enjoyment of pain.

**Traitor** - The protagonist learns to use a new power or weapon. Often the protagonist struggles with the training, creating a question of if they will ever be able to manage the new power or weapon.

**Transformation** - The character magically transforms their clothing or body into something else.

**Transgender Person** - A person who changes to a gender other than the one they were assigned at birth.

**Turned Villain** - An ally of the hero's changes into a villain.

**Twist Ending** - When the ending of the story differs from the expected outcome.

**Two Paths** - Two heroes have differing ideas on how to deal with a villain, causing tension between the heroes. The plans are based on the hero's individual moral codes.

# U

**Unassuming Suspect** - A character that the reader would not suspect of committing the crime.

**Unbreakable Code** - A code that the characters claim cannot be broken, is broken easily by the protagonist.

**Unexpected Inheritance** - The protagonist inherits money or items unexpectedly or from a person that was unlikely to leave them anything.

**Unexpected Parenthood** - The protagonist suddenly discovers they have a child or must take responsibility for a child.

**Unexpected Parents** - The protagonist suddenly discovers they have a child or are responsible for a child.

**Unexpected Pregnancy** - A character discovers they, or someone they had sex with, are unexpectedly pregnant.

**Unrealistic Recovery** - The hero suffers a major wound but moves around as if it was a simple scratch.

**Unreliable Narrator** - The narrator of the story is unreliable which makes the reader doubt their account of the story.

**Unrequited Love** - The protagonist is in love

with a character but does not seek a relationship. Often because the character is in another relationship or expressed that they were not interested in the protagonist.

**Unsympathetic Victim** - The victim has traits or behaviors that make them unsympathetic as a victim.

**Useless Cop** - The character who should be saving the others because of their profession, but fails or is proven to be incompetent.

# V

**Vampire** - An undead creature who usually drinks blood.

**Villain** - A character who does the wrong thing for the wrong reasons.

**Villain Because of Mean People** - The villain's motivation is that people were mean to him.

**Villain Wins** - The villain defeats the hero or the villain escapes.

**Villainous Victim** - The victim is a villain.

**Virgin** - A person who has not had sex.

# W

**Waking Up at the Morgue** - A person who was presumed to be dead, wakes up in the morgue.

**War Obsessed General** - A general who manipulates situations so that he can continue a war or send more troops to a battle.

**War Zone** - The area in a war where the physical fighting happens.

**"We're Not So Different"** - When the villain tries to convince the hero that they are similar people because they have similar traits or desires.

**"We've Got Company"** - A character says this when a rival army or gang is spotted approaching the hero and their allies.

**Wedding** - When two people declare their love for each other formally.

**Weird Girl** - Quirky girl who represents an alternative subculture.

**Weirdo Trope** - A character who intentionally draws attention to themselves by being the weirdest person in the room. Often, they then complain about not fitting in.

**Werewolf** - A character who turns into a wolf. The character has no control over the transformation, which is often triggered by a full moon.

**Western** - Plots and themes focus on the western United States, cowboys, and related concepts.

**Whip of Dominance** - The protagonist has a whip which symbolizes their dominance over the creatures they control.

**White House** - A white building where the President of the United States lives.

**White Savior** - A Caucasian character helps a non-Caucasian character in a way that is self-serving.

**Whodunnit** - A type of mystery story where the characters try to discover who committed a crime.

**Why Choose?** - The female protagonist has two, or more, love interests. Instead of choosing one, the protagonist consensually has a romantic relationship with all love interests.

**Wicca** - An earth-based religion that believes in magic.

**Will They, Won't they?** - The protagonist and a love interest have romantic tension but it's unclear if they will choose to be together or not.

**Wise Old Mentor/ Wise Old Man** - An intelligent older character who guides the protagonist. Often this character dies.

**Wise Villain Speech** - The villain gives a

captivating speech that challenges the hero's beliefs or criticizes society.

**Wise Wizard** - A wizard character who guides the protagonist. Often, this character dies.

**Witch** - A human character that can perform magic spells. This character is often female.

**Wizard** - A human character that can perform magic spells. This character is often male.

**Women and Children Last** - The most innocent members of the group survive to the end of the story.

**Woods** - A setting with a lot of trees.

**Workaholic** - A person who feels a need to work constantly, often sacrificing their family and social life.

**Working Cowboy** - The story focuses on the cowboy's work.

**Workplace** - The location where a character works. This trope expands the office trope to include other workplaces.

**World Doesn't Progress** - The story is set in the future but technology and social structures have not changed from modern day.

**Written by the Winners** - The story is biased because it is being told from the perspective of the people who won the conflict or are the ruling class.

**Wrong Side of the Tracks** - A character who is from a poorer or less desirable area is from the wrong side of the tracks.

# X

No tropes for this section.

# Y

**"You Don't Have to Do This"** - The hero is going to be killed or harmed, and tells their captor they don't have to harm them. Alternatively, the hero is about to do something extremely dangerous and another character tells them there is another option.

**You Wake Up in a Room** - The protagonist wakes up in an unfamiliar room at the start of the story or chapter to add suspense.

# Z

**Zombies** - Non-sentient undead creatures.

# RESOURCES

For more in-depth information about tropes or how to use them, check out these resources

Overly Sarcastic Productions. "Trope Talks." *YouTube/ Overly Sarcastic Productions*, Overly Sarcastic Productions, 2016-2023, https://www.youtube.com/playlist?list=PLDb22nlVX GgcljcdyDk80bBDXGyeZjZ5e. Accessed 27 September 2023.


StudioBinder. "Tropes Explained — Types of Tropes & the Art of Subverting Them." *YouTube*, 26 June 2023, https://www.youtube.com/watch?v=lLcM9mh9sic. Accessed 24 October 2023.


The Tale Foundry. "The Tale Foundry Genre & Tropes." *YouTube/ Tale Foundry*, 24 June 2019, https://www.youtube.com/playlist?list=PLegyBq4Mvn -aXkmtevX1k3VnuHjXLtIwd. Accessed 29 September 2023.

www.ingramcontent.com/pod-product-compliance
Lightning Source LLC
Chambersburg PA
CBHW061253250726
48653CB00002B/648